The Life of Mary for Children

2M

Catholic Classics

Written by
SR. KAREN CAVANAUGH

Illustrated by
WILLIAM LUBEROFF

THE REGINA PRESS
NEW YORK

Artwork © Reproducta NY 1996
Text © The Regina Press

The Life of Mary

Joachim and Anne were Mary's parents. They were so proud of their new baby daughter. They gave her the name Mary which meant "royal incense."

Joachim and Anne knew that Mary was a special gift from God. Soon after she was born, they went to the temple and dedicated her to God.

Mary's mother also taught her how to cook and bake bread. She would help prepare meals and care for the house with her mother, Anne.

Nazareth was a village on the slope of a hill. This was Mary's hometown. Joseph also lived in this town with his family. He was a carpenter.

Early each morning Mary would go to draw water from the well in the center of the village. Here she would meet other young women. All of them came for the day's water supply.

Mary became engaged to Joseph at Nazareth. He was a loving and sincere young man. Every one hoped that there would be a big wedding.

Soon after she was engaged a very special thing happened to Mary. While she was praying, God's angel, Gabriel, came to tell her that God had chosen her to be the mother of the Savior.

An angel also came to Joseph while he was sleeping. The angel told him that Mary's baby was God's child. Joseph would marry Mary, and Jesus would be like a son to him.

Before Jesus was born Mary went to visit her cousin, Elizabeth, who lived near Jerusalem. Elizabeth was also going to have a baby.

Mary stayed with Elizabeth. They thanked God for loving them and for their special children. Mary and Elizabeth had always loved children.

After their marriage, Mary and Joseph decided to make their home in Nazareth. Joseph worked in the carpenter shop and Mary prepared for the new baby. They were learning to be a new family.

Before Jesus was born Joseph and Mary had to go to Bethlehem to register as citizens. They made a long journey and when they arrived could not find a room.

The only shelter that Mary and Joseph could find was a stable in a cave used for animals. Here, Jesus the Savior was born. Mary, his mother, wrapped him in a blanket and placed him in a manger for a crib.

Shepherds came from nearby. Wise men brought gifts from far away places for Mary's baby son. Mary had become the mother of the "new king."

When Jesus was a young boy he lived in Nazareth with Mary and Joseph. Each day Mary cared for the house and did all the cooking and baking.

Once, when they were in Jerusalem for Passover, Jesus got lost. Mary was heartbroken. The next day she and Joseph found him talking with all the teachers in the temple.

As Jesus got older he remained at the center of Mary's thoughts. After Joseph died, Jesus stayed on with Mary. They always talked together and enjoyed each other's company.

Once, at a wedding in Cana to which Mary and Jesus were invited, the wine ran out and

there was nothing to drink. Mary asked Jesus to help. He performed a miracle turning water into wine just because his mother asked him.

Mary's heart broke when she saw Jesus suffer and die on the cross at Calvary. As she bravely stood beneath the cross Jesus spoke and said, "This is your mother." She is our mother and she cares for us.

After Jesus left the earth, his friends and followers stayed together. Mary was very much at the center of this new Christian family. They prayed that the Holy Spirit would come among them.

Because of her love and faithfulness, Mary was crowned "Queen of the Universe." Until the end of time, blessings will come to us if we pray to Mary.

Prayers to Mary

THE HAIL MARY

Hail Mary, full of grace, the Lord is with you. Blessed are you among women, and blessed is the fruit of your womb, Jesus. Holy Mary, Mother of God, pray for us sinners, now and at the hour of our death. Amen.

THE MEMORARE

Remember, O most gracious Virgin Mary, that never was it known that anyone who fled to your protection, implored your help, or sought your intercession was left unaided.

Inspired by this confidence, we fly unto you, O Virgin of virgins, our Mother!

To you we come, before you we stand, sinful and sorrowful.

O Mother of the Word incarnate, despise not our petitions, but in your mercy hear and answer us. Amen.

HAIL HOLY QUEEN

Hail, holy Queen, mother of mercy, our life, our sweetness, and our hope.

To you do we cry, poor banished children of Eve; to you we send up our sighs, mourning and weeping in this valley of tears.

Turn then, O most gracious advocate, your eyes of mercy toward us, and after this our exile, show unto us the blessed fruit of your womb, Jesus.

O clement, O loving, O sweet Virgin Mary.

V. Pray for us, O holy Mother of God.

R. That we may be made worthy of the promises of Christ.

The Rosary

The Rosary is a prayer that pleases Mary. It is easy to learn to pray the Rosary because you know all the prayers by heart: The Apostles' Creed, Our Father, Hail Mary and Glory Be.

The complete Rosary consists of fifteen decades, but is further divided into three distinct parts. Each part contains five decades called the Joyful, the Sorrowful, and the Glorious Mysteries. A mystery is a story about God. The Mysteries of the Rosary symbolize important events from the lives of both Jesus and Mary.

6.

Meditate on 3rd Mystery, saying the "Our Father," ten "Hail Marys" and the "Glory Be."

7.

Meditate on 4th Mystery, saying the "Our Father," ten "Hail Marys" and the "Glory Be."

5.

Meditate on 2nd Mystery, saying the "Our Father," ten "Hail Marys" and the "Glory Be."

8.

Meditate on 5th Mystery, saying the "Our Father," ten "Hail Marys" and the "Glory Be."

4.

Meditate on 1st Mystery, saying the "Our Father," ten "Hail Marys" and the "Glory Be."

3.

Say three "Hail Marys" And the "Glory Be."

9.

Concluding prayers, "Hail Holy Queen" and "Let Us Pray: O God, whose only begotten Son, etc."

2.

Say the "Our Father."

1.

Make the Sign of the Cross, say the Apostles' Creed.

THE JOYFUL MYSTERIES

1. The Annunciation
2. The Visitation
3. The Nativity
4. The Presentation
5. The Finding in the Temple

THE SORROWFUL MYSTERIES

1. The Agony in the Garden
2. The Scourging at the Pillar
3. The Crowning with Thorns
4. The Carrying of the Cross
5. The Crucifixion

THE GLORIOUS MYSTERIES

1. The Resurrection
2. The Ascension
3. The Descent of the Holy Spirit
4. The Assumption of Mary
5. The Crowning of Mary

Our Lady of the Miraculous Medal

This devotion was begun by Catherine Laboure, a French Sister of the Daughters of Charity. She was born on a farm in France in 1806.

She experienced three apparitions of Mary. In one apparition, Catherine saw a picture of Mary standing on a globe with light streaming from her hands. Around the Virgin were the words: "O Mary conceived without sin, pray for us who have recourse to you." Mary entrusted this devotion to Catherine, and told her to have a holy medal made with the picture of Mary, the Immaculate Conception, stamped on it.

As soon as people began wearing the medal, miracles started happening. The medal soon began to be called the "Miraculous Medal."

Catherine never told anyone but her confessor about the visions. So, even at her death in 1876, no one knew that Catherine was the one who brought the Miraculous Medal to the world.

Our Lady of Fatima

One of the most powerful of Mary's apparitions in modern times was to three peasant children near Fatima, Portugal in May of 1917. The three children were Lucia, Francisco, and Jacinta Marta. They saw the figure of a lady brighter than the sun, standing on a cloud in an evergreen tree. They were granted six apparitions between May and October of 1917. Each took place on the 13th of the month, except in August, when the date was the 19th.

On October 13th, when Lucia asked the Lady who she was and what she wanted, she replied with these words: "I am Our Lady of the Rosary; I wish to have a chapel in my honor on this spot. Continue to recite the Rosary every day. People must mend their ways, ask pardon for their sins, and no longer offend our Lord, who is already too much offended."

Her message at Fatima was to accept life's sufferings and continue to pray for the people throughout the world.

Our Lady of Lourdes

One celebrated apparition of Our Lady took place at Lourdes in the southwest of France in 1858. From February 11 to July 16, 1858, the Virgin appeared eighteen times in the hollow of a cave, on the edge of a mountain stream, to a little girl named Bernadette Soubirous, who came from a very poor family.

During the ninth apparition, on February 25, the Lady asked Bernadette to drink from a spring. As none was visible, the child scooped away sand at the back of the cave, knelt, and drank of the water that welled up. The next day a spring was flowing, which produced an abundant supply of water even till today.

On March 24th the Lady said to Bernadette in the local dialect, "I am the Immaculate Conception," and asked for prayer and penance for the conversion of peoples. Mary's request that a chapel be built at the Grotto and spring was fulfilled in 1862.

Our Lady of Guadalupe

On December 9, 1531, the Blessed Virgin appeared on the Tepeyec hill, then about three miles outside of Mexico City, to Juan Diego, an Indian convert.

She told the poor Indian she wished a shrine built there. When Juan Diego told Bishop Zumarraga of the request, he refused to believe him and asked a sign be given.

Three days later, the Blessed Mother appeared again to Juan and told him to gather roses from the hillside, put them in his poor cloak and give them to the Bishop. Though it was December – not the time for roses at all – Juan gathered the roses and presented them to the bishop.

Impressed on the poor Indian's cloak, the bishop saw a picture of Our Lady of Guadalupe.

Guadalupe is one of the great Marian shrines in the world. Pope Pius XII declared Our Lady of Guadalupe the patroness of the Americas.

Our Lady of Czestochowa

The icon of Our Lady of Czestochowa, also known as the Black Madonna, is enshrined on the Jasna Gora (hill of light) above the city of Czestochowa in South Central Poland. Here under this title the Polish people for centuries have honored Mary the Mother of God and her divine Son.

In 1382, the painting of the Black Madonna was brought to the shrine atop Jasna Gora in a monastery run by the Pauline Fathers. The painting was defaced with a sword by thieves, and marks can still be seen on Mary's face to this day.

Since 1656, after the great victory of Poland over Sweden, Our Lady of Czestochowa has been worshiped as Queen of Poland.

The people of Poland have made Czestochowa a center of pilgrimage and the center of their nation. In the years under communist domination the shrine of Our Lady of Czestochowa became the rallying point for the Polish people, who were persecuted for their faith.

Our Lady of Perpetual Help

This title is connected with a Byzantine icon which was stolen from Crete, brought to Rome, and according to tradition (upon the instructions of Our Lady) was placed in the Augustinian Church of Saint Matthew in Rome. After the destruction of the church in 1798, the image was given to the Redemptorists who placed it in the church of Saint Alfonso, built on the same site.

The inscription in Greek above Our Lady means, "Mother of God;" above the child, "Jesus Christ;" above the angels with the instrument of the Passion of Christ, "Michael" and "Gabriel." Jesus looks with fear at the instruments of his future Passion while his little hands are clasped around the hand of his Mother.

Our Lady of Vladimir

One of the most famous and most beautiful of all icons of Mary is that of Vladimir. She is depicted cheek to cheek with the Christ Child, whose arms hold her.

It is a good example of the icon the Russians call tenderness. It was probably painted in Constantinople in the twelfth century, but was first heard of in Kiev, where it was taken in 1155 to the city of Vladimir.

It became famous for wonders and was worshiped as Russia's most sacred image. In 1395, it was enshrined in the cathedral of the Assumption in the Kremlin in Moscow. Several times the Tartars were beaten back under its inspiration and it was carried to critical places in times of distress; the last time to the battlefront during World War I.

Until the revolution, all the tsars were crowned and patriarchs installed in the presence of this image. The Russian calendar commemorates the feast of Our Lady of Vladimir on May 21.

Feasts of Mary

JANUARY 1: Solemnity of Mary, The Mother of God

FEBRUARY 2: Presentation of Jesus in the Temple

FEBRUARY 11: Our Lady of Lourdes

MARCH 25: The Annunciation

MAY 31: The Visitation
The Immaculate Heart of Mary

JULY 16: Our Lady of Mt. Carmel

AUGUST 5: Dedication of St. Mary Major

AUGUST 15: The Assumption of Our Lady

AUGUST 22: The Queenship of Mary

SEPTEMBER 8: The Birth of Mary

SEPTEMBER 15: Our Lady of Sorrows

OCTOBER 7: Our Lady of the Rosary

NOVEMBER 21: The Presentation of Mary

DECEMBER 8: The Immaculate Conception

DECEMBER 12: Our Lady of Guadalupe

DECEMBER 25: Christmas, The Birth of Our Lord